The Burp Book:
Burp it, Belch it, Speak it, Squeak it!

J.B. Davis

Illustrated by: Sean McColgan

1

Copyright © 2013 J.B. Davis

All rights reserved.

No part of this publication may be reproduced,
distributed, or transmitted in any form or by any
means, including photocopying, recording, or other
electronic or mechanical methods, without the prior
written permission of the author, except in the case
of brief quotations embodied in critical reviews and
certain other noncommercial uses permitted by
copyright law.

For permission requests write to:
James@thejamesdavis.com

For more hilarious adventures and shenanigans visit:

www.thejamesdavis.com

Table of Contents

Hi!   6

The Sonic Boom   8

The ABC's of Burping   10

The Choir Burp   12

The Fourth Course   14

Canyon Burping   16

Bully Bombs   18

Burp-Fu: The Brutal Belch   20

Double Trouble   22

The Grumble before the Storm   24

All Grumble, No Rumble   26

Forgotten Food Burps   28

Elevator Burping   30

Communing with Nature   32

Scuba Glubbing   34

The Harley   36

Hiccaburping   38

日本のげっぷ   40

Morse-Code   42

The Never-Ending Story   44

Social Burping   46

The Earthquake   48

Wedding Burping   50

The Squealer   52

Monsters under the Bed   54

Airplane Burps   56

Speaking   58

Trampoline Burps   60

Ventrilaburping   62

Top of the Food Chain   64

Man's Best Friend   66

More Fun Stuff...   68

Hi!

My name is Sean Thunderpants, and for the most part I'm just like you! That's right, I go to school, play video games, love gross stuff (except for vegetables, BLECH!), and have all kinds of fun! The different thing about me is I'm also a level 9 super kung-fu burping master! I've trained since I was born in the noble art of burping and have written this short guide to introduce you to my slightly smelly world. This book is my belching encyclopedia, and while it is in no way comprehensive I know you will enjoy it! I hope you will have fun learning new and exciting (and funny!) ways of bringing amazing burps to everyone around you! Enjoy it as you laugh through the pages… I know I did!

The Burp Book:
Burp it, Belch it, Speak it, Squeak it!

The Sonic Boom

Your belly rumbles like a lion. You
know the burp is coming, but this is no
ordinary burp! You feel your body
shake as the burp travels through it and
erupts. The lion's rumble is now a roar
so loud everyone can hear it! Your cat
flies off into the distance, hanging on
to a tree for dear life as friends fall
backwards while the beastly burp
bellows. You cannot believe it! It
seems this burp will never end! You
sound like a dragon, and are sure fire

will be flying out of your mouth if this carries on. Your cat is flapping in the wind like a flag as others hold onto benches, flag-poles, trees... anything they can get their hands on to not get blown away!

As the burp slowly stops, you and your friends look at each other with wide eyes. You have just lived through a "Sonic Boom!"

The ABC's of Burping

This is an essential tool for any burper. It's the best way to train your belching talents before you move on to the harder ones. Sometimes alphabet burping is harder than you might think because you have to burp each letter to the tune of the alphabet. So it's musical too! If you get really good at it, try ending the alphabet with "Next time will you burp with *mrrrrrp.*" Your friends will love it! If all your friends can do it, try taking turns so each one of you does a letter, then the next person does the next letter. Group alphabet burping is even better! I even got my entire class to burp the national anthem once! It was really fun, but my teacher wasn't very happy.

The Choir Burp

This is a burp for experts only, so start practicing! Other boys and girls may have the voice of angels when they sing, but few possess the burp of a god. You don't have to be a great singer, all you have to do is control your belch! When the notes go up, make your burp all squeaky. When they go down, make it a low, booming burp! Try it whenever you have to sing, or even if you aren't singing! The best musical burps are when no one expects them. Try to find someone singing alone and join in with a belting belch right in their ear. Or, like me, belt a belch when singing in a choir! Last night I quietly mumbled the words to the song we were singing as the rest of my friends sang along, not knowing there was a big bomb brewing in my belly! Finally, the moment came… the big climax of the song! The teacher waved his stick around like a madman and the other children sang louder! Suddenly, a barbarous bellow rang out from within the choir! A musical bellowing burp! As it went on it changed pitch to the song: up and down, stunning everyone into silence! My teacher could only look at me in awe as the first five rows started screaming.

I took a bow and walked off the stage.

The Fourth Course

As all experienced burpers know, food
and drink are the key to a great belch.
A hearty stomach roar is sometimes a
compliment, and other times it is
simply unavoidable. After a full meal,
master burpers can complement the
chef in two ways: The first is a brief
belch to say "thank you." It's a quiet,
quick quip just to let the waiter know
you liked the meal! The second is
much harder, but is a much more heart
(and stomach!) felt thank you. It's a

huge burp that changes smell so everyone knows exactly what food you had! It might sound like a bizarre burp, but if mastered it is the ultimate compliment! I often go to restaurants and wolf down three full courses of fine food and the result is always the same. I can't help but burst out a compliment as the waiter brings the bill! It's only a brief burp but the wonderful smell meets everyone's noses and lets them all know what a great meal I just had! (A lot of people order what I ate because they get a whiff of my belches!)

Canyon Burping

The sweet sound of silence signals the calm before the storm. This type of burp is a rare opportunity, so be prepared in advance by drinking lots of fizzy drinks!

The Canyon Burp is considered one of the natural wonders of the world! My Canyon Burps are louder than the average after-dinner burp, and as my belches echo around the canyon walls they become monsters! Nearby townsfolk look into the sky, expecting a plane to pass overhead! Trees shift in the wind as lizards run for cover! The world hears my cry and tourists smell the stench of soda rising up from the canyon! I have made my gassy mark on the world, and in style. Singers have their huge stages, and burpers everywhere have the Grand Canyon!

Bully Bombs

Not everyone will respect you for your
belching abilities. The school bully
used to pick on me all the time because
of it. That's when I came up with my
secret weapon: Bully Bombs!
Have a breakfast of all the smelliest
burp foods like eggs, peanut butter,
and chocolate milk. When you unleash
the breakfast burp he won't know what
hit him! Just remember, the smellier
the foods you eat and the bigger the
burp, the better it will be! With a belly

full of burping potential you can walk right up to the biggest bully in school and he will scream like a little girl! (He might even give you his lunch money too!)

Burp-Fu:
The Brutal Belch

To be a master of Burp-Fu you must master your belch. This art requires you to train daily, but you must be committed! Scoffing down full meals and drinking gallons of soda are just a few of the trials you need to endure to master The Brutal Belch. This extremely difficult burp takes lots and lots of practice but it is worth it, promise! You know when karate guys break bricks with their bare hands?

The Brutal Belch means you can do it with your bare burping talents! It's a burp of concentrated fury and power that can break just about anything in your way. Locked door? No problem! Wall in your way? No worries! The Brutal Belch makes life so much easier; it's an essential life skill that all burping masters must have.

I trained for weeks, conquering the art of burp control and power. My Master held up my test; a thick plank of wood. I closed my eyes and urged my body to produce what was needed. My body shook and with a roar I unleashed a bold and booming burp! The wood snapped in half and my Master staggered backwards in surprise. I bowed to my Master as the stench of The Brutal Belch filled the room.

Double Trouble

The Double-Trouble requires stealth, control, and cunning. Although difficult to master, the Cover-Up is an effective method for tricky double trouble disasters. When a rear-ender is imminent you need to act fast! Just like I learned to do. Don't panic! As one smelly rocket rushes one way, you need to produce a breathtaking belch right on cue! If you mis-time it by even a second the gaseous goo may be blamed on you. You need to have control over both cheeks in order to sneak out a stinker while blasting out a burp.

The belch needs to be just loud enough to cover up the sound of the fart, so judge how loud it is going to be and belch accordingly. I know I know, it's tricky but you'll get the hang of it. Remember that you can always blame the dog if you get caught. Get it right and you've just gotten away with a Double-Trouble!

The Grumble
before the Storm

Sometimes your body lets you know
when a monster burp is on the way
with what I call The Grumble before
the Storm. This little rumble lets you
know a giant gassy belch is heading
your way.

Your tummy always starts things off,
hardly making a sound, but you'll hear
it if you listen real close. Pretty soon it
gets a bit louder and your belly will
start to shake just a bit. Next come the

full wobblies with your whole tummy rumbling and shaking all over the place! People around you will start to notice you now as the ground starts to shake (and you should probably warn them by screaming "RUN FOR YOUR LIFE!")! At this point, my tummy always grumbles and rumbles like eighty-two cats are trapped in it and my belly starts shaking all over like my burp can't find a way out! My face and lips all wobble as I belch out a beauty that looks really funny.

Be careful though, these can turn into All Grumble, No Rumble's!

All Grumble, No Rumble

Alas, not all burps live up to the build-up! I might be a top trumpeter of belly bombs but not all my belches are knockouts. Burpers and Burpettes of all ages and experience will sometimes suffer from the "All Grumble, No Rumble." This is when you think you are going to do a brilliant belch and it comes out sounding like a hiccup! You might think you always know when a big burp is on the way but sometimes you can be wrong. Burps can be very misleading!

I pride myself on knowing when a brilliant burp is on its way so I always gather a crowd to marvel at my mastery, but burps betray us from time to time. This will happen, but fear not! The best belches sneak up on us too!

Forgotten Food Burps

If you need more reason not to trust burps let me introduce what I call Forgotten Food burps! Burps might trick us sometimes and turn out to be an All Grumble, No Rumble, and other times they turn out just like this... Nasty! I'm sad to say it's usually too late once you can tell a Forgotten Food Burp is on its way. The smell, the taste, the angry growling in your tummy. Too late! You're having leftovers for dinner! The Bully Bomb bombed you!

The emergency routine is to first recognize that it is a Forgotten Food burp. The next step is to RUN! Find the nearest restroom you can before you end up like poor me! Even master belchers cannot stop the Forgotten Food Burp. Just be careful and try to spot these as soon as you can to save yourself from a sticky (and gross) situation. Tacos should only be eaten once!

Elevator Burping

Soon to be an Olympic event, Elevator
Burping is a tough sport. I have trained
my entire life for these kinds of
situations! In order to be a champion
Elevator Burper you need to get a
bedazzling belch ready before you get
in the elevator. The elevator should be
full of people too, because the more
people the more points. Once the doors
slide shut, the game begins! You have
until the first person gets out to
bamboozle everyone in the elevator

with your burping talent, so there's a time-limit!

The first set of points is awarded for the number of people in the elevator. One per person, so the more the merrier! The next set is for how loud the belch is and how it rates on the Smell-O-Meter: Loud is great, smelly is good, both are a perfect 10! The final points are for people's reactions... I made someone cry one time! It was the proudest moment of my life.

(For extra fun try burping in glass elevators!)

Communing
with Nature

Masters of the burping world often
spend time in the wild talking with the
animals through belching. It is a
difficult art to do, but as with all burps
it can be done through practice and
determination! I like to spend time by
the pond with frogs to learn their ways
and hear them ribit. After much
practice and hard work, when I burst
out a riburrrrrp the frogs now think I'm
one of them! They all start ribit-ing

along, making a baffling burp-tastical musical! Burping in the wild can be a lot of fun, and while frogs might be the best belchers in the animal kingdom, which animals can you try to get to burp along with you?
(Did you know that the first ever "super belch" came from a frog?! I've even heard that's how the first ever pond was made! Respect the frogs!)

Scuba Glubbing

What many people don't know is that burping is something you can do anywhere… and I mean anywhere. I told you about burping in the wild, but I like to take burping to the extreme! Scuba diving might be fun, but Scuba Glubbing is a whole new activity. This is basically burping beneath the water, brilliant! Belching out bubbles under the sea and seeing them rush up to the surface looks awesome! Just hold your breath, swim underwater and release a

Kraken burp! From above the water all people will see is bubbles, and if they listen close they might just hear a faint burping noise. You look a bit like a burping shark to everyone else with a burping bubble trail! I put on my goggles (so I can see my handiwork) and swim underwater with the fish and burst out a burp. The fish might swim away, but if you ever see a shark just squeeze out a belch and he will leave you alone. Blowfish are the burpers of the sea though, they puff up all big and release giant bubbly burps! Watch out for them!

The Harley

I might not be old enough to ride a motorcycle yet but I can sure make my bike sound like one! Next time you are out on your bike try burping so loud it sounds like a Harley revving up its engine. Your friends will be really impressed! The Harley burp needs to be a big one, but more importantly it needs to sound just like a Harley. It needs to be loud, but it needs to go like Buuuu-burrrr-burrrrrp so it sounds really cool. Stepping up the booming belch as you change gears makes it sound even cooler! Nothing beats the feeling of riding my bike, wind flowing through my hair, and doing a Harley burp! When you ride past people super-fast they won't be able to tell the difference as you roar away. Another top tip: if you aim your burp behind you it makes you go even faster, just make sure it's a big one! So get your friends together, put on some shades and a cool jacket and become part of my super-cool Burping Biker Gang!

Hiccaburping

We all get hiccups (I think they're just little burps) that we can't stop from happening. We all get burps that we can't stop from happening. So The Hiccaburp is when you hiccup and burp at the same time! It makes such a weird noise and it feels really odd. It's like a war between hiccups and burps to see who will win!
Hiccups attack and attack and never stop while burps barrage them with blasting belches. It's a crazy battle,

and it's all coming out of my mouth!
There are so many wonderful and
different kinds of Hiccaburps, too
many to count. I had one where I was
blasting out a burp and then I
hiccupped and the burp stopped. I
guess the burp didn't like that very
much though, because the next time I
had hiccups a little burp popped up
every time! It was weird.
I think everyone has had The
Hiccaburp when you burp and hiccup
right at the same time. It makes a
really funny noise and it always makes
me laugh.

日本のげっぷ

Everyone thinks burping is rude, but I'm only trying to be nice! I've spent years searching for friends who can appreciate a good belch. Well in Japan we burpers are heroes! It's actually considered rude NOT to burp after you eat! The Japanese really have the same love for belching that I do. They know that a big burp is the only way to show you enjoyed your meal… it's only polite! So after you wolf down all these new and exciting foods, let 'er rip! The louder the burp, the bigger the compliment to the chef. I think Japan might have to be my new home!

I went there and after loads of weird and wonderful foods, we all let out a beastly burp. Since it is a compliment in Japan to belch after a nice meal, it would be rude not to let loose a bold, barrage of burping compliments! When you're in restaurants or in someone's house and you want to let them know you had a good meal, unleash the burping beast within! (Did you know they swallow live goldfish?! I could feel them swimming around in my belly! I had drunk lots of fizzy drinks so I guess I shouldn't have been surprised when one of them let out a belch so big it shot me three feet up in the air! Weird!)

Morse-Code

Sometimes you need to send top secret messages to other stealthy burpers. That's where Morse Code Burping comes in, the super-secret code for covert burpers! If you see a couple of guys burping to each other it might be a top secret conversation... Keep your eyes peeled! You will need to practice your belching skills to master this one. If you want to say "soda" then that would be burpburpburp burp burrrpburpburrrrrrrrrrrrrrp. Just make sure you remember to do the longer belches and the shorter ones otherwise you might be saying you like vegetables. So like I said, you need to practice burping lots and quickly to say the right things! Try it with your friends and see if you can have top secret conversations with them! People around you will just hear burping, but you will hear the messages. They might smell your lunch but the smells don't give away your secrets!

The Never-Ending Story

The Never-Ending Story is, well, a burp that never ends! It can start off as any kind of burp and it just doesn't want to stop! These might not be the loudest, but they are definitely the longest of all the different types of belches. Big burps can become huge belches that never seem to stop! Little burps can get out of hand and last for hours! I once burped for five days straight! (I had drunk so many fizzy drinks bubbles were coming out of my nose!) I just ripped out a monster I couldn't control!

Belches can have a mind of their own, starting off small and then going on forever and ever and ever. Any burp can do this, but the bigger the belch the harder it is! When I feel a Never-Ending Story happening I try my best to stop it, but these burps are sometimes the best kind. Sometimes you can't help but lose control and let the belch run wild and free!

If you ever try to go for a super-mega-burp-roar make sure you time it! See which one of your friends can burp the longest!

A word of warning though: It might be impressive and one of your best burps ever, but there is only so much burping and belching your tummy can take before it becomes a Forgotten Food burp! Blech!

Social Burping

Sometimes a little, polite burp is needed. If you feel a bit of a belly rumble and don't want to release the jungle then go with a simple Social Burp. Use it at funerals, when applying for college, or even when talking to the president. (We all know the president loves burping too, but if your burp suddenly turns into an Earth Splitter then you might have accidentally started World War 3! Before you know it planes would be flying overhead and battleships would be sinking... Burps would fire from guns and giant clouds of smelly belches would cover your town! Best go with a social burp to be safe…)

Remember, the social burp is only a little one! Keep it polite and respectful…

Okay, let's be honest, there's only so much Social Burping I can take! Sometimes I am dragged to parties that are SOOOOOOOO boring and I watch people stand around for hours just talking! I always think that what these people need is a good BELCH! The key is to watch others… as soon as one person lets out a burp the game is on! Sure, most people will let out a little "merp," and I TRY to play along… but eventually there's only so much I can take! If no one's talking to me it's only polite I show off my talent! I do a little squeaky burp ("excuse me"), then I let one roar. People may not look impressed, but I know they're just jealous… It's hard to be so talented.

The Earthquake

Remember how I said burps can get out of control? Well Never-Ending Burps can sometimes turn into Earth Splitters! These kinds of belches can start earthquakes, split roads and bring down buildings! Breathtaking and brutal burps like the Earth Splitter can be dangerous, so be careful! I once wrecked my whole town! After a little burp blossomed into a booming belch cracks opened up everywhere, like the Grand Canyon was opening in my town! Hey, maybe that's how the Grand Canyon was made?! Beware belchers, burps bring bamboozling and baffling things. The bottom line is be careful! I wrecked my whole neighborhood. Don't make my mistake!

Wedding Burping

Weddings are a very special day for loving couples. It's a day dedicated to their undying love for each other... right? Wrong! Weddings are your opportunity to be a burping celebrity and bring a bit of fun into everyone's lives! Just unleash a breathtaking belch and steal the show! It's especially fun if there are songs, because you can become a star in the beautiful world of belching by adding a few Choir Burps! It is true that bellowing burps in The

Grand Canyon might feel great, but it doesn't gain you fame like Ring Bearer Burping. I was the ring bearer at a wedding and the whole church was silent apart from the priest who was saying stuff about love (boooooring!). I went to give the rings and after they took them I took my chance! With a huge grin I let out a bold and booming *BRRRRRRRRP!* The belch echoed all around the church making it sound awesome! "Bravo!" said the priest (even though everyone else didn't look very happy). I took a bow to the stunned crowd and walked off. I'm sure they will tell my story for years to come!

The Squealer

Ever wake up to what sounds like a spider screaming? Don't worry, it was just a little midnight burp making its way out of your belly! I used to think there were cockroaches playing frisbee under my bed until I finally remembered I had a soda two hours before I went to sleep. I hate cockroaches.

One time I actually let out a midnight roar so loud my cat got stuck to the ceiling! I tried to get it to come down but its claws were so sharp and it just wouldn't let go. My cat looked really funny upside down with all his hair standing straight up. It actually gave me an AMAZING idea for one of my all-time favorite burps: The Monster under the Bed!

Monsters under the Bed

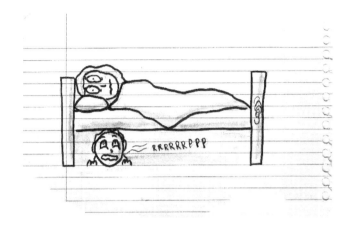

RRRRRRPPP

Want to really scare someone? I
suppose you could hide in their closet
and jump out, but I have a better idea!
First off, hide under their bed and wait
until they are almost asleep. This is
where the fun begins! As they are all
tucked up in bed, slowly drifting to
dreamland, they hear something. What
was that noise? Was it the bogeyman?
Where is it coming from? Little do
they know it's you under their bed
letting out a big burp! First, they'll

hear your tummy growling and grumbling (which is scary enough!), but then it gets fun… As you let out a monstrous beast of a belch they'll scream in fear because a monster is under their bed! Of course, it will only be you but they won't know that. I suggest you try different kinds of burps because some are better than others. If you make your burp sound like a ghost then that will be even better. Careful though, if your burp is too scary you might get ghosts joining in! (It's not the bogeyman coming to get them, it's the burpeyman!)

Airplane Burps

Burping 30,000 feet up in the air feels amazing! Flying through the sky, belching like a dragon, it's a lot of fun! But you have to be careful! You might be eager to begin blasting out burps but watch out through security. Bellowing belches can scare security officers, and you don't want lots of massive, muscled guys chasing after you! Once you're up in the air, release the belch! You can part clouds for the plane and even make the plane go faster by burping backwards and belching your way home! Have fun on the way to wherever you're going… just remember that you can burp to avoid boredom too. I hear that when the President steps off a plane he releases a roar to make sure people know he has arrived!

Speaking

Like I keep saying, burping is for everywhere, anywhere, any time. Be it in the sky or just when you're talking to your friends, there is never a bad time for burping! Out-of-the-blue belching is sometimes the best kind because people are so surprised! You might be talking about your favorite film, what your gross sister said, or your favorite video-game! I like to buy tickets while burping (*"one pleauuuurp"*) or quote my favorite

58

movies: "I am your father," and, "I'll be back-*urrrp*," are some of my favorites. Try it out!

Burping impressions are always funny too, and it doesn't just have to be films. Try doing impressions of your friends or your parents when they tell you to "Stop *burrrrrrp*ing!" Just make sure you don't do it so loud that they can hear you!

Trampoline Burps

Step one, chug a full soda as fast as you can. Step two, bounce away! In no time you will have created a brilliant burping mixture with all that fizz jumping around inside you. So once you have the perfect barrel of belching power ready, let rip! Bounce and burp! Belch as you jump, belch as you land, burp away! If it's a big enough burp you will jump really, *really* high! You'll have fun bouncing up and down and belching away, but want to know

what is even better? Burping backflips!
Burping as you tumble and spin
through the air, bouncing and belching
is so much fun. Just beware, all the
fizzy soda and bouncing means that
sometimes it might be a bit more than
just a burp!

Ventrilaburping

You know how ventriloquists can throw their voice so it looks like the puppet is talking? You can do this without the puppet and you don't have to talk. You can burp! You can make it sound like anyone, or anything, is burping! You could make it sound like your dog's burping, your mom, your sister, your friend, anyone!
I like to do this at restaurants. I spot a couple out on a date, chatting away, and boom! I make it sound like the guy

blasted out a massive belch! The woman's face is always so funny, I have to try my best not to laugh and give myself away as the guy tries to explain it wasn't him!

If you try making it sound like your dog is burping, that always confuses people too! Everyone always says, "I didn't know dogs could burp!" Practise and try it out yourself!

Top of the Food Chain

Animals need to be reminded who's boss! And what is the best way to do that? Roaring like a lion, but with a burp! It needs to be the loudest, meanest, biggest burp imaginable! Humans might be at the top of the food chain, but we need to let the animals know why. Belting out a beastly belch lets all the animals know why we are still king of the jungle. I like to hike up into the woods and boom out a burp. You will see all the animals scurrying away as your belch rings out through the trees. Deer and squirrels and hedgehogs and all manner of creatures will go running as you roar.

Sometimes we just need to let all the wildlife know who's the biggest beast in the jungle!

Man's Best Friend

Sometimes we might have to remind the wild animals who's boss, but at home it can be a lot more fun. If you have a dog, or if your friend has one, and it barks at you, burp back! The closer you can make it sound like a bark, the better! I've sat for ages with my dog barking at me, me belching back at him. If you can actually make it sound like a burping bark, your dog will get really confused. He'll be wagging his tail and barking non-stop, just keeping barking out the belches! If it's a bigger dog, just unleash a bigger burp! Belch it out between you and find out who really is top dog!

More Fun Stuff...

If you liked the funny shenanigans in this book then please rate it well!

Stay on the lookout for more adventures of the infamous

Sean Thunderpants
at:

www.thejamesdavis.com

Sean will be back with more fantastic burping, belching, and barking madness before you know it!

Until next time…

Have fun burping!

Sean Thunderpants

13726671R00041

Printed in Great Britain
by Amazon.co.uk, Ltd.,
Marston Gate.